# Bride and Blades:
## How to Survive a Surgical Marriage

# Dr. A. H. Yurvati

Yurvati Legacy Press
www.yurvatibooks.com
info@yurvatibooks.com

# Table of Contents

# Dedication

This book is dedicated to my lovely wife, Sharon. Without her guidance, encouragement and love, I would not have had such a successful career. She has been the foundation of our successful marriage for over 50 years.

# Acknowledgements

I want to thank Melissa Gannon, my artist, for doing a stellar job of the book jacket. Olivia at Writers' Branding and the team at Reading Glass Books.

# Prelude

There is as saying that a surgeon has two wives. The "legal wife" and "surgery wife". Both require attention and expectations from their spouse.

At times, they can be in opposition. Attendance at a special event is expected by the "wife" and the "surgery wife" interferes by requiring presence at an emergency surgery.

At times, the stress and strains of life can result in a negative relationship and divorce. Interestingly, the "surgical wife" survives.

This book is intended to be a guide for pre-med, medical students, residents and new attendings as they transition through the major milestones of life and at the same time preserving a successful marriage. The book is divided into six major parts:

Part 1: Married prior to medical school
Part 2: Married during medical school
Part 3: Married during residency
Part 4: Married after residency
Part 5: Married and life changing events later in life
Part 6: Reflective Takeaways

# Part 1

# Married Prior to Medical School

A stable marriage prior to acceptance into medical school carries a better prognosis than a tenuous relationship. Brian Wu on student doctor net wrote an article describing the variables in marriage prior to medical school (Wu, 2016, student doctor net). American Association of medical Colleges estimated that 10% of pre-med were married and their mean age was 27.

Married pre-meds had more encouragement and support in dealing with MCAT, Applications and admissions interviews. Having a dual income greatly stabilized the relationships. One variable that can be plus or minus is children, especially the number. There is the add stress of excelling as pre-med and balancing family life. Strong relationships working as a team greatly stabilize marriage. Other family support such as parents living nearby can reduce stress as they can be caregivers, babysitting or visiting.

| Items to Consider | | | |
|---|---|---|---|
| Marital Support | Manage household | Prepare meals | Shopping |
| Time Management | Schedule Household Duties | Date Nights | Prioritize Time Together |
| Financial | Dual Income | Savings | Debt |
| Family Planning | Number of Children | Time Between Births | Family Support |

An important issue is debt prior to matriculation. High debt will be a burden carried over, unless the spouse is employed. According to the AAMC, the debt across racial/ethnic groups, most had no premedical education debt; however, significant percentages of matriculants from some groups had $25,000 or more in such debt, including Black or African American matriculants (40.5%), American Indian or Alaska Native matriculants (30.5%), Native Hawaiian or Other Pacific Islander matriculants (26.0%), and Hispanic, Latino, or of Spanish Origin matriculants (24.0%).

Across racial/ethnic groups, most had no premedical education debt; however, significant percentages of matriculants from some groups had $25,000 or more in such debt, including Black or African American matriculants (40.5%), American Indian or Alaska Native matriculants (30.5%), Native Hawaiian or Other Pacific Islander matriculants (26.0%), and Hispanic, Latino, or of Spanish Origin matriculants (24.0%).

Figure 10. Amount of premedical education debt for U.S. medical school matriculants by race/ethnicity, academic year 2018-2019.

Click on legend item below to add or remove a bar from the report.

- ● American Indian or Alaska Native
- ● Asian
- ● Black or African American
- ● Hispanic, Latino, or of Spanish Origin
- ● Native Hawaiian or Other Pacific Islander
- ● Non-U.S. Citizen and Nonpermanent Resident
- ● Other
- ● Unknown
- ● White

Note: The numbers reflect responses to the following Matriculating Student Questionnaire (MSQ) question: "Do you have any outstanding educational loans for your college/premedical education?" The totals in each race/ethnicity category include all individuals who selected that category, alone or in combination with any other category.

Source: AAMC Matriculating Student Questionnaire data as of March 22, 2019.

*Reproduced from AAMC Matriculating Student Questionnaire, March 22, 2019.*

## 15 Signs You Are in a Stable Relationship & Ways to Maintain It

Draven Porter, 26 September 2024 from Marriage.com.

You can always tell when a couple is in a stable relationship. When you look at them together or apart, they appear satisfied, relaxed, comfortable, and happy. A stable relationship makes both partners thrive as individuals and enjoy their time together as a couple.

So, you can see when in the company of people who are lucky to be in such a relationship.

Yet, this isn't something given only to the lucky few; all of us can work on our relationships and turn them into a thriving and motivating force in our lives.

Stable relationships, however, are much more than just looking happy. Stable relationships do not mean that there are no ups and downs in the marriage, but it is more about how much understanding there is to manage these ups and downs.

### What is a Stable Relationship?

A stable relationship is one that is 'stable,' and does not cause you to question where the relationship is going, what it is, or what it means to either of you. What is stability in a relationship, or what is relationship stability, you ask? It is when you and your partner have a baseline for your relationship, where it should not waver from, it is considered a stable relationship. A stable relationship also means that if you waver from this baseline, you work healthily and together to come back or as close to the baseline as possible. A stable relationship is also one to have explicit trust and healthy communication.

## Why is stability important in a relationship?

A relationship is a mix of various factors. Most people are often found looking for passion, stability, and emotional health in a romantic relationship. Some people also believe that passion and stability in a relationship are exclusive to each other.

However, that might not be completely true. A passionate relationship can also be stable. But if a choice between a passionate relationship and a stable relationship arises, what will you choose?

In that case, stability in a relationship may be more important than passion. Passion may eventually fade away or not give you the same 'high' as it does in the beginning. However, stability can help your relationship thrive and sustain all the highs and lows, proving way more important than passion in the long run.

## 15 Signs You Are In A Stable Relationship

Here are some signs that your relationship is stable.

## 1. You show your feelings to each other

This means not only love and affection but anger and frustration as well. Stable relationships are not characterized by the absence of disagreement or discontent in some situations.

Happy couples are still humans and experience negative emotions like the rest of us. But, unlike in unhealthy relationships, partners in a stable relationship have an assertive way of communicating their feelings. That means they don't withdraw, aren't passive-aggressive, or plain aggressive for that matter, and don't repress their emotions.

They express their discontent explicitly but respectfully and lovingly and work on the issues as a couple (not as boxing partners, as usually happens in toxic relationships).

And this is something that works in both ways – not only does a stable relationship promote such healthy expression of the entire range of emotions, but if you start communicating your needs and views in an assertive manner, the relationship might also turn for the better.

## 2. Couples support each other's growth as individuals

If you think of a person that you consider is in a stable and healthy relationship, you probably have a feeling of being in the presence of a fulfilled person, someone who is not only a part of a couple but is also a self-accomplished individual.

Unlike in unhealthy relationships, partners in stable relationships feel confident and safe. As a result, they don't feel insecure when their partner is trying new things, advancing their career, or learning a new hobby.

When partners are insecure about each other and their partner's commitment, they spend all their energy and train themselves to keep their partner as close as possible.

And their partner also can't thrive in such an unsupportive environment and often might become an underachiever.

But when partners are confident, they tend to be very supportive and enthusiastic about their loved one's growth and eager to share their new experiences – which leads to the next shared characteristic of all stable relationships.

## 3. Partners constantly reconnect and rediscover each other

And this is partly done by discussing one's passions, interests, and newly learned skills and experiences. By sharing their inner world with their partner and by talking about how they spend their day (in detail, not just "Yeah, it was all right"), those in stable relationships keep rediscovering each other.

And, when one changes, as it inevitably happens with time, the other partner is not left out but was there for the process and gets a chance to adapt.

Another way to reconnect each day is to touch each other in a non-sexual way, which is something couples in a stable relationship do all the time. This means hugging, holding hands, and just touching and being close.

Interestingly, apart from sexual intercourse, which can both be pushed aside or remain a vital component of even unstable relationships, it is almost a rule that if a relationship is erratic, these signs of affection almost vanish.

## 4. They work on their marriage and love all the time

It may sound dull to those accustomed to unpredictable and "exciting" relationships, but this is a sign of both partners being emotionally mature enough to develop a genuine and healthy attachment. So, what does work on a relationship look like?

It's implementing all of the above, and also being open, providing reassurance to your partner about your relationship, using your social life to provide additional support to the relationship, and also seeing commitment as a positive thing in which responsibilities that come with it are something to be accepted with joy.

Being in a stable relationship is not something that just happens (or doesn't). It takes some effort to learn to develop as a part of a couple, but when you get it right, it's the most rewarding experience possible for a lifetime.

## 5. Partners are best friends

In a stable relationship, both partners are each other's best friends. However, a stable relationship also means your partner is not your only best friend. You have more friends, and your partner is also one of them.

One of the signs of stability in a relationship is that the basis of the relationship is friendship. You are friends first and lovers or spouses later.

When the relationship is based on friendship, it is stable because you feel you can trust each other explicitly, tell each other everything without judgment, and love each other irrespective of the flaws.

## 6. You can let go of fights and disagreements

Another sign of a stable relationship is when both of you can get over, and let go, of disagreements and fights. This is because you can see where your partner is coming from, understand their point of view, and know that their intentions are always right.
Dionne Eleanor shares,

*During conflict and disagreements, it's not about who's right or wrong but about understanding each other's perspectives and moving forward together.*

## 7. You rely on each other

Reliance is another sign of a stable relationship. A relationship is stable when you both can rely on each other. You must trust your partner to do things right or count on them to be there for you when things are not the best or the relationship can be stable. In a stable relationship, partners know that their spouse has got them, no matter what.

## 8. You do not try to be right

Arguments or disagreements in relationships are okay. While the two of you may not see eye to eye on something, you do not care about being right or even trying to be the right one in a disagreement. You understand that one of the signs of a stable relationship is that it is the two of you against the problem and not the two of you against each other.

## 9. There are no toxic signs

Another sign of a stable relationship is when there are no signs of toxicity in a relationship or marriage. This means that you do not gaslight each other, treat each other badly, or give each other silent treatments. This helps your relationship stay healthy and stable.

## 10. You are both predictable

This does not mean you are bored. Being predictable means you both know how the other person will react in any situation. Another sign of stability in a relationship is when you are both predictable but not boring and only for each other.

## 11. You fight fair

Another sign of a stable relationship is when you fight fairly. When the two of you disagree or argue, you do not make it dirty. You do not bring up things that are not needed in this fight and only bring up solutions that can help.

## 12. You speak each other's love language®

Love languages® is a popular concept. In a stable relationship, you both understand each other's love language and try to express your love in a way that your partner understands and feels loved.

## 13. You are involved in each other's lives

Another sign of a stable relationship is when you are involved in each other's lives. This means that you take part in each other's decisions, give your opinion about things that matter, and give each other advice to help a situation.

## 14. They stand up for you

Couples in a stable relationship have each other's backs and stand up for you. Whether in a social setting or a family gathering, they will speak up for you in case the need arises.

## 15. You have couple rituals

How to become stable in a relationship? Have some couple rituals.

Another sign of a stable relationship is when you both have rituals as a couple. It could be simple – such as a weekly date night, or something grand such as an exotic weekly vacation.

If both of you have been around each other for a long time, long enough to have rituals, your relationship is most likely stable.

## Three things make relationships stable?

Three things that make a relationship better are **trust, communication, and love**. Stability in a relationship is a by-product of these factors in a relationship. Trust, communication, and love can make a relationship better in every way.

Sharon and I have exhibited or experienced these tenants of a stable marriage. I will never forget a discussion we had early in our relationship. We were on a date and talked about many things. Then, she asked me, *"What do you want to do with your life?"*

I responded not sure probably stay in the Army for 20 years, become a paramedic. She gave me a stern look and said, *"You need to become a doctor."*

I responded I was told I was not very smart, so I don't know if that's possible. With that response she said, *"Well, if you're not going to try, I won't marry you."*

The rest is history; I did become a doctor. I correct myself by doctor time 3! A Medical degree, a PhD and a Doctor of Science. We focused on my attainment of a medical degree, as a team we worked to fulfill this dream. I could not have accomplished this goal without her help, guidance and a lot of nudging times.

Once we were discharged from the Army, we enrolled at California State University, a state supported school with reasonable tuition and our GI Bill. She had an associate's degree and finished her B.S. in two years, then a Masters in two additional years. I completed my B.S. in four years and started applications to medical school. I had multiple interviews and acceptances; we decided on the Texas College of Osteopathic Medicine (TCOM). I was an out of state student, only 10% of the class could be out of state. The tuition was $1500/ year, in my fourth year it increased to $5,100. We were able to stay out of debt, and save money, and were able to do vacation trips.

| Takeaway | | |
|---|---|---|
| Stay Focused on the goal | Admission to Medical School | Team effort |
| Finance | Plan how you will pay tuition and living expenses | Average tuition $238,420, or $59,605 per year |
| Family Planning | Personal choice, variable demand on time away from studying | Family support |
| Wellbeing | Plan vacation prior to starting medical school | Couple only have family baby sit, you need to solidify your connection |

**How we planned:**

We were married for seven years prior to matriculation. Sharon completed her bachelor's in nutrition and while enrolled in her master's program worked as a consultant, this brought in additional income. I took the California R.N. board examination to be a Registered Nurse, working part-time at Kaiser Permanente first in the E.R. then as a weekend supervisor. In addition, I found a teaching position at an LVN school in downtown LA, with more additional income. We placed in savings, had no credit card debt, only car payments.

I applied to multiple schools and started to receive invitations for interviews, this was costly, however we had saved for this. Next, I received offers of acceptance, I chose a state supported school as the tuition was very low. In addition, the school had strong financial support, and was in a very safe area.

I accepted the seat at the Texas College of Osteopathic Medicine in Fort Worth, Texas. At that time, I was a California resident, so I was considered "out of state". By Texas statute only 10% of the class can be non-resident. So, we were off to Texas to start another chapter of our life together.

# Texas College of Osteopathic Medicine
Camp Bowie at Montgomery • Fort Worth, Texas 76107 • (817) 735-2000 • Metro 429-9120

March 22, 1982

Albert H.Olivencia-Yurvati
18561 Prairie # 3
Northridge, California 91324

Dear Albert:

On behalf of the college, we are pleased to offer you a
position in the 1982 entering class of the Texas College of
Osteopathic Medicine.

To accept this offer, you must respond in writing to this
office within ten days of your receipt of this letter. A
non-refundable assurance deposit of $100.00, check or money
order payable to the Texas College of Osteopathic Medicine,
must accompany an acceptance of this offer. An additional
$150.00 is due on or before 1 June 1982. The total non-
refundable deposit of $250.00 will be applied toward your
first year tuition.

Your admission to TCOM is contingent upon 1) your completion
of all academic and course distribution requirements, including current course work, at a level of performance equal
to that at the time of application; and 2) our receipt of
all official transcripts, no later than 1 July 1982, from
all colleges and/or universities you have attended.

Should you not be able to meet these requirements, it is
your responsibility to contact the Admissions office. If
you have any questions, or if there is any way in which we
can be of help, please do not hesitate to contact us.

We commend you for your academic performance and for your
interest in health care. We look forward to working with
you and serving you in your continued growth and develop-
ment.

Sincerely,

Earlene McElroy
Director of Admissions

EM/bw

Under the direction of the North Texas State University Board of Regents

20

# Part 2

# Married During Medical School

Getting married during medical school can be challenging. The hours devoted to studying and the stress of examination after examination can be stressful on newlyweds. The best time to plan a marriage is between the first and second year. Next would be prior to the third year after Level 1 boards. The final would be in the fourth year after the residency match, the uncertainty of residency and location of training is resolved. Some authors recommend getting assistance from families in planning the wedding will reduce the pressure associated with wedding planning.

The AAMC (American Association of Medical Colleges) has reported that 10% of beginning medical school are 27 years old, and there is an increase rate of students who marry during medical school. Being married while in medical school offers some advantages for dealing with the rigors of medical school. One advantage is the emotional support and understanding of the demands of medical school. Having a spouse can assist with the management of the household, have a prepared meal at the end of a long day. Married students report that they have better time movement, prioritization of time and protecting a date night once a week, helps with overall well-being.

There have been several reports citing the disadvantages of being married to a medical student. Stress and time constraints can strain the relationship. Balancing the demands of medical school with the demands of marriage can be overwhelming. Missing birthdays, anniversaries and family events can also take an emotional toll.

If one spouse is a student then the other becomes the financial supporter, if both are students then this makes the financial demands more complex. Therefore, family support and student loans are essential, as student debt can exceed $225,000.

Another consideration is family planning, as major adjustments will need to be made. Medical schools do not traditionally provide maternity provisions, so the student will have to request a leave of absence, which will extend their medical education. The added stressors sometimes prevent the wife from completing medical school. Other considerations are financial, for example the wife is working, while the husband is a student. Now that income is deleted, requiring further student loans and increasing the debt ratio, which could impact credit scores.

## Takeaway Timing for Marriage

| YEAR 1 | Avoid high intensity course examinations |
| --- | --- |
| YEAR 2 | Summer break between Year1 and Year 2 |
| YEAR 3 | Avoid due to starting rotations |
| YEAR 4 | After Match Day Now you know what residency, institution and city you will be moving to |

It's been reported that the divorce rate can approach over 50% if married during medical school. Their reason is the hospital becomes the home: the home becomes foreign. The spouse feels abandoned due to the number of hours and years of missing the spouse. Married couples who are both in the medical field do better, many times they are at the same institution and get to see each other more frequently.

# Part 3

# Married During Residency

Residency training is the most intense and demanding phase of a physician's life. Duty hours, night calls, unexpected add-on cases and additional after-hours meetings. Although the Accreditation Council of Graduate Medical Education (ACGME) adopted the 80-hour work week depending on the specialty, it can still be exhausting. Couples need to ensure they understand these demands to successfully hold a marriage together. Surgical residencies specifically have unique stress on the marriage. Add on cases, unanticipated complicated cases that prevent breaks or nutrition. Once the day is completed, exhaustion sets in and the spouse who has been waiting all day for some quality time is disappointed as the resident falls asleep while sitting on the couch.

Open communication and active listening go hand in hand. Communication helps in understanding each other's perspectives and improves emotional status.

Active listening will assist in resolving conflict, validates feelings and can strengthen the emotional bond.

The hardest items are time management and quality time. Scheduling "date nights", no phone, or other distractors, just each other. This simple strategy may save a marriage.

Another stressor occurs in the last year of training. Go into practice institution, private or hospital system? Or additional fellowship training.

Will require relocation of the family, children will need to enroll in a new school system. Other considerations are contracts, length of employment, compensation and benefits. Recent surveys indicate a trend towards shorter initial job tenures for physicians, including surgeons, who have recently completed their residency or fellowship. While the average for all practicing physicians at their first post-training job is around 6 years, for those who finished training since 2018, this average drop to less than 2 years. This suggests that newly trained surgeons may be changing jobs more frequently early in their careers than in the past.

The next challenge is finding apposition either private practice, employment by hospital or academic. Academic positions often pay less, but there is a reward for training students and residents. Being a mentor is priceless. An added benefit is fixed monthly income and benefits. Private practice can be challenging depending on the group. Salary can be variable month by month depending on productivity. Hospital system employment can be a hybrid of fixed income versus productivity.

Surgeons have diverse employment opportunities in various settings, including private practice, hospitals, academic institutions, and government programs. While demand for surgeons, particularly general surgeons, is projected to remain high, some reports predict a shortage by 2025. Surgeons can work in hospitals, ambulatory surgery centers, or even in the military. The specific role and setting influence salary, with general surgeons earning an average of $423,000 annually in 2023, according to Weatherby Healthcare.

Pros and cons of joining a surgical group practice Joining a surgical group practice can offer numerous advantages and disadvantages for surgeons.

## Pros

- Shared administrative burden: Group practices typically share administrative tasks like billing, scheduling, and office management, freeing up surgeons to focus on patient care.

- Established patient base: You'll likely inherit an existing patient base when joining an established group practice.

- Enhanced negotiating power: With more partners, the group can negotiate better rates with insurance companies and other third-party providers.

- Financial stability and potential: Joining an established group can provide financial stability, and for partners, a share of profits and potential for long-term growth, according to Panacea Financial.

- Collaboration and peer support: Group practices foster a collaborative environment, offering opportunities for peer consultation, mentorship, and learning from colleagues, potentially improving competency levels.

- Improved work-life balance: Sharing call duty and vacations with other surgeons can lead to a more predictable schedule and better work-life balance compared to solo practice.

- Potential for specialized teams: Larger groups may be able to form dedicated operating teams with specialized training, potentially leading to improved patient outcomes and efficiency.

- Access to technology and resources: Group practices may have better access to and resources for expensive equipment, technology, and specialized staff that might be unaffordable for solo practice.

- Reduced risk: Financial and clinical risks can be shared among group members, limiting individual liability.

## Cons

- Less autonomy: You might have less control over practice decisions, including income distribution, office management, and patient care policies.

- Potential for conflict: Disagreements can arise over practice changes, patient referrals, or other issues, requiring effective conflict management skills.

- Less influence on practice policies: Policies and procedures are typically set by the group, potentially limiting your ability to shape the practice culture.

- Dealing with other's patients: You may need to treat patients you are unfamiliar with, which can sometimes be met with hesitancy by patients, according to Hospital Recruiting.

- Potentially lower initial income: While offering stability, the initial income in a group practice might be lower compared to the potential earnings of a successful solo practice.

- Limited control over income distribution: Your say in how income is distributed might be limited, especially as a new member.

In summary, joining a surgical group practice involves weighing the advantages of shared resources, stability, and collaboration against potential limitations in autonomy and income. It's crucial to assess your priorities and find a practice that aligns with your professional goals and values.

# Part 4

# Married After Residency

Many couples choose to get married after completing residency due to the demanding nature of medical training. While some may choose to marry during or before residency, others find the financial and time constraints of residency make it more feasible to wait until after. The decision often depends on individual circumstances and preferences, with both options having their own set of pros and cons.

**Advantages of Marrying after Residency:**

- **Financial stability**

    Residency is often a period of lower income and higher expenses, making it challenging to manage the costs of a wedding and early marriage. On average, medical school graduates in the United States carry a substantial amount of student loan debt.

Here's a summary of the figures from recent reports:

- Average Debt (including undergraduate pre-medical education): Around $264,000.

- Average Medical School Debt (alone): Approximately $200,000.

- Average Debt for Graduates in 2023 (medical school-related): $202,453, according to the Education Data Initiative.

Important Considerations:

- Debt Varies: These are averages, and individual debt amounts can vary significantly depending on factors like:

    - Attending a public versus private institution.

    - The duration and type of residency training.

    - The extent of premedical debt.

    - Personal financial circumstances and resources.

- Impact on Career Choices: The burden of medical school debt can influence future career decisions, particularly for those considering lower-paying specialties like primary care.

- Loan Repayment: Managing this debt often involves navigating various repayment options and understanding factors like interest rates and loan forgiveness programs.

In essence, while pursuing a career in medicine can be rewarding, it often comes with a significant financial commitment in the form of student loans.

## Reduced stress:

Residency is a demanding and stressful period and adding wedding planning to the mix can be overwhelming.

## More time to focus on career:

Marrying after residency allows doctors to focus on establishing their careers without the added pressure of a new marriage.

## Greater flexibility in wedding planning:

After residency, couples often have more time and resources to plan their wedding without the constraints of a busy residency schedule.

## Advantages of Marrying during Residency:

- **Strengthened bond:**

  Some couples find that navigating the challenges of residency together strengthens their bond and relationship.

- **Shared experiences:**

  Sharing the residency experience can create a unique connection and understanding between partners.

- **Potential for emotional support:**

  Having a partner during residency can provide valuable emotional support during a stressful time.

- **Potential for early family planning:**

  Some couples may choose to marry during residency if they plan to start a family soon after.

Important considerations:

- **Communication is key:**

  Regardless of when a couple chooses to marry, open and honest communication is crucial for navigating the challenges of residency and marriage.

- **Shared expectations:**

  It's important for both partners to have a clear understanding of each other's expectations and priorities.

- **Flexibility and adaptability:**

  Residency is unpredictable, so couples need to be flexible and adaptable to changing circumstances.

- **Support systems:**

  Having a strong support system for family, friends, or mentors can be helpful for both partners.

Hold off on expensive cars and home. Payoff educational debt and improve credit score.

Here's a breakdown of key information about credit scores:

1. What a credit score is and why it's important

- Definition: A credit score is a three-digit number, typically ranging from 300 to 850, that summarizes your credit risk.

- Impact: Your credit score influences your access to financial products like loans and credit cards, and the interest rates you'll pay on them. It can also affect rental applications and insurance premiums.

2. Factors affecting credit scores (using FICO as an example)

- Payment History (35%): Your record of on-time and late payments is the most significant factor.

- Amounts Owed (30%): This includes your total debt and how much of your available credit you're using (credit utilization).

- Length of Credit History (15%): The longer your history of responsible credit use, the better.

- New Credit (10%): Applying for too much credit in a short period can negatively impact your score.

- Credit Mix (10%): Having a variety of credit accounts (e.g., credit cards, loans) can be beneficial.

3. Credit score ranges

While different scoring models exist, FICO and VantageScore are the most common. Here's a general guide to the range:

- Excellent: 800-850

- Very Good: 740-799

- Good: 670-739

- Fair: 580-669

- Poor: 300-579

Divorce (*We hope you don't need to go here*) is an emotional and complicated process for anyone, but for doctors and other medical professionals many unique complications can arise that require special attention. A doctor's personal and financial future may be seriously impacted by the outcome of a divorce, as his or her medical license, ethical standing, and professional career will be put under a microscope during the divorce process. If you're a doctor and are considering a divorce, the following guide is for you.

## 1. Hire an experienced divorce attorney that is Board Certified in Family Law.

Many doctors choose to be represented by their healthcare or corporate counsel in their divorces. They may also hire the first attorney they find on the internet. Just like doctors, attorneys specialize in certain areas of practice and hiring someone without experience in family court or with divorce will be detrimental to your case in the long run. Texas is a community property state, meaning that all property and income accumulated during the marriage by spouses in the marriage belong jointly to the couple. This can include real estate, professional practices, trusts, LLCs, businesses, employment benefits, retirement accounts, and stock options. Family law attorneys are familiar with representing doctors and know about the complex earnings and property ownership of various related professional items, including private physician's practices.

## 2. Disclose everything to your counsel – do not leave anything out.

Doctors, and other clients, often fail to be candid with their lawyers and do not disclose bad behavior or problems that may arise during the divorce process. This can be detrimental and have serious consequences. Withholding information – including the existence of an affair, funds spent on illegal substances, problems with a medical practice, and drug or alcohol abuse – will prevent your attorney from doing their job. Attorneys who are aware of all potentially damaging information can often neutralize it and make sure that it does not derail the divorce process.

## 3. Obtain an accurate valuation of your medical practice.

The valuation of a doctor's medical practice or the interest they hold in a practice is frequently a contested issue during a divorce. Doctors may understate or overstate the value of their practice or of their interest in practice. When it comes to the valuation of medical practice, one must distinguish between personal goodwill and commercial goodwill. In Texas, personal goodwill does not possess value and is not considered an asset. Commercial goodwill relates to the practice's reputation and its ability to attract and retain patients. Commercial goodwill can potentially be considered an asset during divorce and an experienced divorce attorney will know how to work with experts to appropriately value it for property division purposes.

## 4. Insist on a confidentiality agreement.

Many doctors fail to ask for a confidentiality agreement to protect their patients and other confidential or proprietary information related to their practice. This could include financial or other business information that if misused could damage the doctor's reputation or practice. Confidentiality agreements can limit the spread of information to certain people involved in divorce, which protects a physician's patients and practice.

## 5. Adhere to all deadlines and requests for information – even if you are busy at work.

Being a doctor takes an immense amount of time and energy. Focusing on patients is the number one priority, however, do not let that prevent you from meeting all required deadlines during the divorce process. While gathering documents and meeting with your divorce counsel may be a low priority compared to treating patients, deadlines must be met for the process to be finalized in a reasonable amount of time. Disregarding deadlines and requests for documentation can only make the experience more difficult for everyone involved and could result in monetary sanctions.

## 6. Try to set realistic expectations.

Doctors going through the divorce process often have unrealistic expectations of what the outcome of their divorce might be as well as how long a divorce can take. Every divorce is unique and the complexity and timeline for each will revolve around your specific circumstances. What a friend, family member, or coworker went through in their divorce is not what you will face. Discuss the possible range of outcomes with your divorce attorney and try to be open and accept their estimated timeline for the process.

## 7. Spousal support may get complicated.

Divorce involving doctors tend to also involve high net worth estates. Larger marital estates can be complex and involve many different investments and other financial holdings. This matters greatly when determining spousal support and property division. One spouse will often support the other financially during their time at medical school, which must be considered when determining spousal support and in the division of the estate. Medical school debt may also complicate the issue as well.

## 8. Prioritize caring for your children.

Doctors may not be able to have as active a role as stay-at-home parents as caregivers for their children, given many have busy and unpredictable schedules. Make sure to not only spend time with your children but also to be prepared to schedule daycare, take kids to school, go to parent-teacher meetings, and more. Also have a plan for childcare if you are called to the hospital in the middle of the night for a medical emergency. Having reliable childcare contacts and plans will be essential to maintaining full or partial custody of your children.

### 9. Be prepared to rely on experts.

Sometimes, experts will be needed to testify during divorce proceedings. Some examples may include a certified public accountant, therapist, or appraisers. You and your lawyer will likely need to retain the services of these experts early in the process, so they are available if necessary.

# Part 5

# Married and Life Changing Events Later in Life

You are finally practicing surgery and have a great life. Beautiful home and the means to take vacations. Then, you are suddenly faced with life-changing events that disrupt your career and income. The best way to deal with this situation is with pre-planning. Ensure retirement contributions, so you have income to replace what you have lost. Consider downsizing your home to reduce expenses. We faced the challenge when Sharon developed urachal adenocarcinoma and required a partial cystectomy. She retired from her position as bariatric consulting dietitian. Then, she had a massive stroke with residual expressive aphasia. The next change was my multiple myeloma, requiring chemotherapy and back surgery. Followed by a 360 corpectomy with the third lumbar vertebrae replaced with an implant. Spinal neuro stimulator and pain pump. This required me to semi-retire, close surgical practice, but was able to come back as academic Chair of Medical Education Health Systems Science, research lab, and surgical core clerkship director. Coming back part-time gave us some extra income. We also had a retirement 401k, to pull funds from, as well as downsizing from 6,000 square foot home on two acres, to 3,250 square feet on a half-acre. This downsizing reduced expenses for utilities, etc.

Good news, we pre-planned and have the funds to maintain our lifestyle. Our credit score is excellent, and we pay off credit cards to zero balance.

We have also been able to give back to my medical school scholarships and participate in fund raising. We have endowed a significant estate gift to the University. I feel it's important to give back and assist the students who come behind you.

# Part 6

# Reflective Takeaways

Open communication.

Agree on family planning.

Always remember important occasions: Birthday, Anniversary, Christmas, Valentines Day.

Going away to conference, always leave a card at the bedside for every night gone, with a short note.

If you have children, get family to take care of them so you can enjoy an "adult" vacation.

Always be faithful, avoid temptations for an affair, doctors are a favorite prey for house wreckers!

*Avoid the Cougar!!*

# Epilogue

I hope you will find this guide valuable as a part of your professional journey as a surgeon. My intent was to lay out practical advice, that perhaps can save good marriage and reduce the divorce rate amongst surgeons.

All royalties will be designated to the American College of Osteopathic Surgeons Medical Student section via the Trust Fund.

# Biography

Albert H. Olivencia-Yurvati, D.O., PhD, DSc(*hc*), DFACOS, FACOS, FICS, FAHA, CPPS

Albert H. O-Yurvati, DO, PhD, DSc, DFACOS, FACOS, FICS, FAHA, is a 1986 graduate of the University of North Texas Health Science Center, Texas College of Osteopathic Medicine. He completed his Internship and General Surgery residency at Tulsa Regional Medical Center at Tulsa, Oklahoma, and served as Chief Resident his final year. He then completed a residency in Cardiothoracic and Vascular Surgery at the Deborah Heart and Lung Center, Robert Wood Johnson Medical School at Browns Mills, New Jersey, where he also served as chief resident. He is AOA board certified in Cardiothoracic-Vascular and General Surgery, and he is a fellow of the American College of Surgeons as well as the International College of Surgeons.

Other educational activities include a Graduate Certificate from the University of North Texas Toulouse School of Education in Teaching and Adult Learning. He completed a PhD in Education from Northcentral

University with a concentration of Organizational Leadership.

Currently, Dr. O-Yurvati is a Professor Emeritus and Chair of the Department of Medical Education Health Systems Science at the Texas College of Osteopathic Medicine, and he is also Professor of Integrative Physiology in the School of Biomedical Sciences at the UNTHSC. He is a Visiting Professor at the University of Strathclyde, in Glasgow, Scotland, in the Department of Biomedical Engineering. Granted a Doctor of Science (*hc*) from the University of Strathclyde.

He has received numerous awards from the UNTHSC, most recently including the 2012 Clyde Gallehugh DO Memorial Award, the 2011 President's Award for Clinical Excellence. He also received Doctor of Philanthropy in 2011, and in 2010, he was the recipient of both the Benjamin L. Cohen Award for Outstanding Research Achievement and the TCOM's Dean's Award for Philanthropy. In addition, he has been awarded two Academic Commendation of Excellence (ACE) Award for superior post-tenure reviews.

He is certified by the Institute of Healthcare Improvement with a designation of CPPS (Certified Professional Patient Safety).

Dr. O-Yurvati has served on many committees on the local, state, and national level. He is Past President of the Metro Fort Worth American Heart Association and is a past Board member of the Texas Affiliate of the AHA.

He also received the AHA Distinguished Service Award. On a national level, Dr. O-Yurvati was the chairman of the American Osteopathic Board of Surgery. He is actively involved in numerous committees of the ACOS, and he has served as a discipline chair and representative to the Board of Governors, as well as cardiothoracic educational program director. He has received the Orel Martin medal, Guy Beaumont Educational Award and the Ballinger Distinguished Surgeon Award. He is a Distinguished Fellow of the ACOS.

He is on the editorial board of the *JOA* and *Filtration*. He is a reviewer for many peered journals to include *Cardiovascular Research and Experimental Biology and Medicine*, *Annals of Thoracic Surgery*, and the *JOA, Perfusion* and *Cureus*.

Dr. O-Yurvati has published over 100 peer-reviewed articles, three book chapters, numerous abstracts, and three books. He is the recipient of over 2.5 million in grants, to include NIH, NASA, DOD, and Osteopathic Heritage Foundation funding. He is a Primary Investigator in multiple Phase 2 and 3 clinical trials. He lectured nationally and internationally, and he has presented previously at the Therapeutic Filtration and Extracorporeal Circulation meeting at the prestigious Hammersmith Hospital in London, England. His research interests include the inflammatory effects of cardiopulmonary bypass, cardiac metabolism, mechanical cardiac assist devices, and machine perfused organ preservation, and patient safety.

# Published Books

Available on AMAZON. All royalties go to UNT Health Texas College of Osteopathic Medicine (TCOM) Scholarship Fund and the University of Strathclyde General Scholarship Fund.

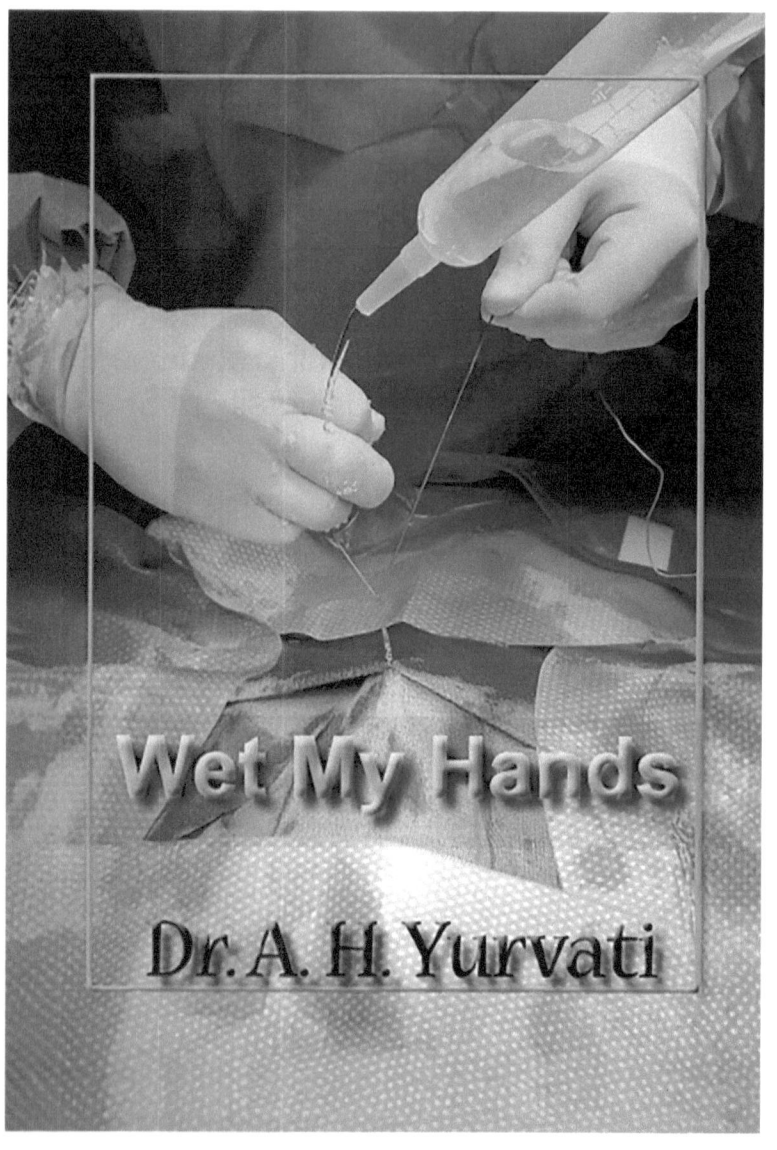

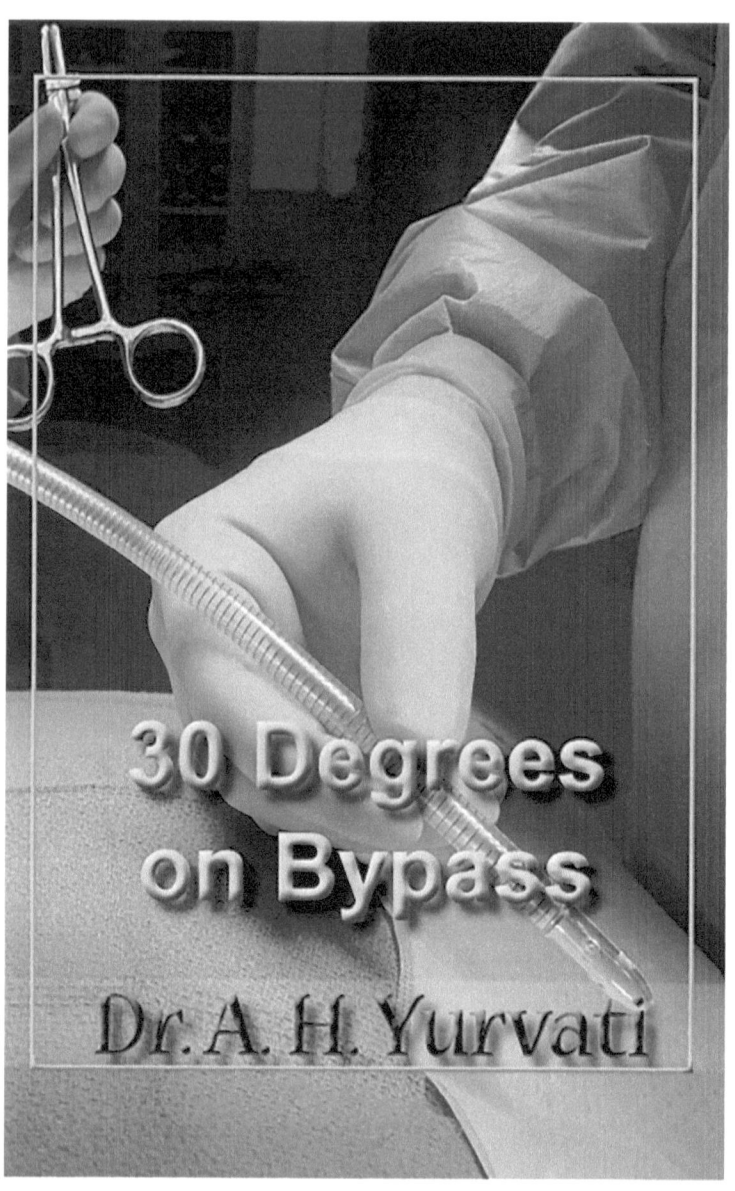

www.ingramcontent.com/pod-product-compliance
Lightning Source LLC
Chambersburg PA
CBHW031237120626
46545CB00003B/1165